KITCHEN BREWING

Jakob Nielsen and Mikael Zetterberg
Photography: Fredrik Ottosson

hardie grant books

EASIER THAN REPAIRING A PUNCTURE, HARDER THAN BUYING BEER!

Everyone can brew

It's been six years since we decided it would be fun to hang out by brewing beer. We had watched YouTube videos with Americans brewing beer. It looked fun, and didn't seem all that difficult. And in the videos they said the beer tasted really good. So we ordered the raw ingredients and equipment and, one afternoon, we got started in Mikael's basement. Twelve hours later, in the small hours, we had finished our first brew. Our eyes were stinging and our enthusiasm was gone. We realised that the people in the YouTube clips were 1) good at brewing beer and 2) good at editing videos so that brewing beer looked completely straightforward. Brewing beer was not easy. No. The first bottles went straight down the sink.

But since beer brewing was also an excuse for us to hang out at each other's houses (despite no longer being kids), we carried on experimenting. We watched even more videos of brewing Americans and improved our home brewing skills. For a year, Thursday evenings were dedicated to brewing beer. We tested different brewing methods in a sort of battle to find the easiest way to make really delicious beer. Eventually, we arrived at a method we wished had existed when we had started out. Our socialising project soon turned into a starting-a-business project: The Little Kitchen Brewery. The company's purpose was to get more people to brew their own beer as easily as possible using as little equipment as possible. Most importantly – the beer had to taste really great. Every time.

Until recently, home brewing had largely been about fiddly equipment and very difficult instructions. We hate . . . well, we don't like, equipment and difficult instructions. We like it when just about anyone can create something that feels great. Something you want to serve to your friends and family.

There are lots of good books about how to brew beer, and how to take the next step in home brewing. Our intention with this book is to fill a gap that ensures that everyone has a sporting chance from the off to brew really good beer. Kitchen brewing is a small step for a beer brewer, but a giant leap for mankind. Extreme hyperbole, but you get the point. Time to brew, enjoy and, hopefully, brag. Good luck!

Jakob and Mikael

WHAT'S KITCHEN BREWING?

Kitchen brewing is about turning traditional home brewing from something pretty difficult and time-consuming into something easy and fun, without losing any quality along the way. Traditional home brewing is more suited to those who are willing to dedicate most of their spare time to Googling brewing equipment, the anatomy of beer making and how on earth you put together a recipe for the perfect smoked porter*. Those who just want to brew a good beer should direct their attention to kitchen brewing. You can see what sets kitchen brewing apart from traditional home brewing on the next page.

* There's nothing wrong with traditional home brewing – it's fun too!

Volume

A kitchen brewer brews smaller volumes than a home brewer. In this book, the recipes produce 4–5 litres (8½–10½ pints) of good beer, which is the equivalent of half a crate. This means you can brew everything yourself, and that everything is just that little bit easier. Instead of a 30-litre (65-pint) plastic fermentation vessel, which is best kept out of sight in the garage, you use a handy glass carboy (demijohn), which can be put on the shelf as an ornament when you're not brewing. The smaller volume also means you get a good quantity of beer. Traditional home brewing usually results in around 70 bottles of beer. That's a lot of beer. And it's an incredible amount of beer if you've just brewed a smoked porter that you're not that satisfied with. The final 69 bottles of just-okay smoked porter won't be worth serving to others or drinking yourself. Kitchen brewing our way provides 12 to 14 bottles of beer to enjoy. Completely manageable.

Time

In home brewing, it's normally known as a 'brew day' when it's time to brew. Sounds wonderful! But after trying out traditional home brewing, we've discovered that this is because it takes an entire full-length day to brew like this. Kitchen brewing takes a total of 2–3 hours.

Simplicity

The smaller volume means you can use equipment you already have in your kitchen. Most people have a few saucepans, a kitchen strainer, a ladle and a funnel. Apart from a little brewing equipment, this is all you need to get started.

Creativity

Kitchen brewing is also about creative joy. You don't get into kitchen brewing to achieve a lower price per bottle. No, it's about an outlet for your creativity and the feeling of creating real beer. You might even come up with a name and make your own label for the beer.

Where to draw the line?

When are you a kitchen brewer, and when are you a home brewer? For some (like us), kitchen brewing is enough. You try out new beer styles, you brew IPA in the summer, stout in the autumn and winter, and a lager for midsummer. Maybe you take a recipe you like and add a new flavour (pistachio, anyone?). Others set the bar higher. They want to produce the perfect lager, or have their sights set on getting their beer into the shops. They can't help but read up on what happens to all the sugars during the mash phase. Or how the yeast really behaves at different temperatures. If that's you, then you long ago crossed the line that separates kitchen brewers and home brewers. We wish you the best of luck! We'll be here under the kitchen extractor fan.

EQUIPMENT

Open the kitchen cupboards and get out two (or even three!) 20-litre (42-pint) plastic buckets with lids, two 10-litre (21-pint) saucepans and around 50 glass bottles. Only joking. No normal person has kitchen cupboards that big. Or that equipment*. The great thing about kitchen brewing is that it works just as well in a kitchenette as it does in a full-size kitchen in a detached house. While you do need *some* equipment, it will definitely fit into your kitchen cupboards.

* Once again, there's nothing wrong with traditional home brewing – as we've already said, it's fun too!

What you probably already have

A funnel, a kitchen strainer, a whisk, a large saucepan, a medium saucepan and a ladle. If you're an eager kitchen brewer, that's all you need to pull out of your kitchen cupboards. Hang on! A pair of scissors is also handy when it comes to opening the bag of hops. And a standard 10-litre (21-pint) plastic bucket can be useful for disinfecting your equipment.

What you probably need to buy

In addition to what you already have, you'll probably need to spend £60–80 ($85–115) to become the complete kitchen brewer. There are two ways to do this. The most comfortable is to go online and buy a ready-made beer home brewing starter kit that contains everything you need. Googling 'beer starter kit' will be the toughest part of the process. The second way is to source all the equipment yourself. You can see what you need overleaf.

The great thing about brewing equipment is that it can be used more or less forever. If you invest well, you'll never need to buy any more equipment. However, it is crucial that you clean it all after every brew so that bacteria and other dirt don't contaminate your equipment and cause some unpleasant aftertastes in your beer. Once you've got your equipment, the fun begins: deciding what your first brew will be.

Brewing equipment

1. fermentation vessel, e.g. a 4–5 litre (8½–10½ pint) glass carboy (demijohn)
2. silicone stopper that fits your fermentation vessel
3. fermentation lock
4. thermometer – a normal kitchen thermometer will do
5. siphon, which is just a plastic or silicone pipe
6. bottle caps
7. bottle capper
8. disinfectant, e.g. Saniclean or Star San

7.

6.

8.

HOPS, MALT, YEAST AND WATER

Raw ingredients

The whole thing is quite simple. To brew beer you need hops, crushed malt, yeast and water. The malt consists mostly of barley, which can be roasted for differing lengths of time. The longer it has been roasted, the darker it is in colour, which makes the beer darker too. The malt also contains sugar, which is released when you put it in warm water. Once the sugar has dissolved into the water and the malt has given it colour and a little flavour, you season it with hops. Hops also bring bitterness and contribute other flavours. If beer tastes of something like passion fruit, citrus or mango, it's usually the hops that have brought it about. When the brew is done, you cool the beer and add yeast. Once in the fermentation vessel, the yeast starts to do its job. Yeast is crazy about sugar and eats up the sugar released by the malt at the start of the brewing process. Once the yeast is saturated with sugar, it shows its gratitude by leaving behind alcohol and carbonic acid for the beer. And that's how you make beer.

As always with raw ingredients, it's important to keep an eye on the expiry date. Yeast normally keeps for about a year. Hops are best stored in their packaging in the freezer. This usually ensures that hops keep for around 6 months. It is also important to use fresh crushed malt. The older your crushed malt is, the less effect it has during the mash, which is when the sugar is released from the malt.

The thing that makes beer more exciting than any other drink is that you can keep varying the ingredients – forever! Do you want your hops flowery, or perhaps earthier? European or American? Do you want smoked or very hard roasted malt? Or perhaps you fancy wheat malt? When you think you know everything there is to know about malt and hops, you'll actually only be about a tenth of the way through the anatomy of beer. Then it's time to learn about how different types of yeast, fermentation times and temperature impact the beer. You can also learn about how the pH value of your water affects the beer and how you can control this to optimise the taste. But we're definitely not going into that in this book.

We've chosen to use American hops in most recipes, which give a fairly fruity flavour and aroma to the beer – the kind of taste most people love. If your response is that you don't want 'some bloody fruity beer', then it's because you've not tried it (source: empirical research). In this book, we exclusively use hop pellets instead of hop cones. We also use two different types of base malts: pale ale malt and pilsner malt. But to give some beers a little more character and colour, we have sometimes complemented them with black malt, chocolate malt and caramel malt. The first two are suitable for stout, while the latter is great for an India Pale Ale or American Pale Ale. Another important ingredient in our recipes is spraymalt, a practical product for kitchen brewers. Spraymalt is an unhopped, dried malt extract that gives the beer a more full-bodied flavour. We've also chosen to use dry yeast in all recipes, partly because it keeps for longer in the fridge than liquid yeast, but also because it is easier to use. All you have to do is cut open the bag and pour the yeast into the wort (see page 106).

BUY ONLINE
Buy all your raw ingredients online. Visit one of the major sites and you won't go far wrong.

NOTE
Ensure that all the malt you buy is crushed so that it is easy for you to follow our recipes.

Raw ingredients

1. yeast
2. crushed malt
3. water
4. pellet hops
5. spraymalt

2.

1.

3.

5.

4.

BASIC METHOD

Anyone can brew our recipes without prior knowledge. They are based on the same basic method, which we call kitchen brewing. If you get to grips with it, you'll be able to brew all the recipes in this book without any trouble. What separates the recipes are primarily proportions, temperatures and cooking times. These are specified in each recipe.

In brief

It's fine to kitchen brew on your own, but it's more fun if you do it together with someone. As a rule, the brewing takes 2–3 hours, including getting everything out, putting it all away and doing the dishes. About the same time as it takes to bake bread. Once the brewing is done, the beer needs to ferment in the fermentation vessel. This usually takes about 2 weeks, depending somewhat on room temperature and how much sugar there is to ferment in the vessel. After fermentation, it's time to pour everything into bottles, at which point the carbonic acid forms with the help of the yeast and sugar, which takes another fortnight. In total, it'll be around 4 weeks before you can remove the cap and pour yourself a glass of really good kitchen brew.

Over the next few pages, we describe each phase in the basic method and how to go about it. Let's get started!

You will need:
Brewing equipment

fermentation vessel

fermentation lock

silicone stopper

thermometer

disinfectant

ingredients

Kitchen equipment

1 large saucepan, minimum 5 litres (10½ pints)

1 medium saucepan, 2–3 litres (4–6 pints)

ladle

kitchen strainer

funnel

whisk

scissors

10-litre (21-pint) bucket

a few cool packs

¹. Preparation

Hygiene is vital in all types of brewing. The cleaner you keep everything, the less risk there is of flaws in the flavour. Additionally, you can store the beer for longer if you have taken care in relation to hygiene. There are two simple steps. First, wash away all dirt. Be very careful to wash away any leftover stew or anything else from saucepans, and any wort in your fermentation vessel. When all surfaces that come into contact with the brew are free of dirt, it's time for the second step – disinfection.

Everything that comes into contact with the brew after boiling the wort needs to be free from bacteria. This sounds more difficult that it actually is. You pour a little disinfectant into a bucket with water and submerge the things you need bacteria-free for as long as the instructions on your disinfectant state. To disinfect anything that won't fit in the bucket, such as saucepans and the fermentation vessel, you should pour some diluted disinfectant into them and shake the liquid around. One other tip is to disinfect the unopened yeast packet and your scissors.

Many people get unnecessarily stressed out by the cleaning. Stay calm. It's all very easy. Once the wort has finished boiling, it's important that everything it comes into contact with is clean and free from bacteria. Before it's boiled, it doesn't matter whether it's bacteria-free as the heat kills all the bacteria. When everything is clean, it's time for the next step – mashing.

sfeminismen

s ännu – tyvärr

LARS R

Stads
en u
åter

> Cindy Sher-
> mans estetik
> ekar allra star-
> kast i Grzeszy-
> kowskas ska-
> pande.

kvinn
för ett

ack

Mash resting.

Separating the mash between two saucepans.

². Mashing

Mashing might not sound all that pleasant, but it is! When you pour the malt into warm water, the kitchen is filled with more or less the same smell as when you bake bread. Turn on some music, because you've got a couple of hours of fun ahead of you.

Do the following: Heat 1.7 litres (4 pints) of water in one of the saucepans to between 68–78°C (154–172°F) (see each recipe). Pour in all of the crushed malt and stir. Take the saucepan off the heat, put the lid on and leave to stand for about 15 minutes. During this stage, it's best if the temperature remains constant, which means it may be worth wrapping a towel around the saucepan to keep it warm. After 15 minutes, you have what is known as 'mash' in the saucepan.

³. Separation

The process of separating the crushed malt from the liquid in the mash through filtration is known as lautering. For the first time, you'll have an idea of what your beer will be like. You can now see roughly what colour the beer will be.

Do the following: Put a kitchen strainer on the empty saucepan. Pour the mash and all liquid through the strainer. This means the crushed malt is captured by the strainer, while the liquid ends up in the saucepan. Move the strainer with the malt to the now-empty saucepan and pour the filtered liquid over the malt bed and into the saucepan. Repeat this pouring between the saucepans three to four times. Between each filtration, you should rinse away the malt residue from the saucepan that has just been emptied. Eventually, you will have removed all the goodies the crushed malt has to offer to make the beer look and taste great. You should now have about 1 litre (2 pints/4 cups) of liquid (known as 'wort') in your large saucepan.

⁴. Boiling

Now the beer is really beginning to take shape and it's time to season the wort with hops, which give it bitterness, flavour and aroma. In our recipes, we use hop pellets. Our favourite moment is cutting open the aluminium bag of hops and getting a real hit in the nose from the smell. Enough about that. Let's carry on.

Do the following: Dilute the wort with cold water to bring the total volume of liquid in your saucepan to 4.5–5 litres (10–10½ pints) (see each recipe). Put the saucepan on the heat and turn it up as high as it will go. While the liquid is being heated to 100°C (212°F), you should pour in the spraymalt. Use an ordinary whisk to mix the spraymalt into the wort. Wait. Watch. Boiling this quantity of liquid takes a while. Once the brew is at the boil, it is usually time to add the first batch of hops. Be careful as there is a risk it may boil over as you add the hops. Depending on the recipe, you may have to add the hops in several batches.

⁵. Cooling

We're not going to lie: cooling is the new version of watching paint dry. But make the best of it and pour yourself a beer while you wait. Once the beer is at room temperature, you can finally add the yeast. The boiling is over and it's important that everything that will be in contact with the beer from this point on, such as the thermometer, is bacteria-free.

Do the following: Put the cool packs in your sink followed by the saucepan, making sure it is stable. Fill the sink with cold water – almost enough to make the saucepan teeter. Monitor the temperature constantly until it is about 20°C (68°F). Now, it's time to ferment.

⁶. Fermentation

It's often said that brewers make wort, yeast makes beer. That's probably true, but nevertheless this is a pretty fun phase – the final stage of the brew. You have to shake the yeast around in your fermentation vessel and then put the stopper back in.

Do the following: Put the funnel and strainer in the mouth of your disinfected fermentation vessel, then pour the beer from the saucepan into the vessel as carefully as possible. The strainer will catch hop residue while the beer flows into the vessel.

Next, add the dry yeast. A half bag of dry yeast is sufficient for 4 litres (8½ pints) of beer. Properly reseal the yeast packet and save for another brew. Disinfect your hands and tightly grip the bottom of the fermentation vessel with one hand while putting your other hand over the open mouth. Firmly shake the vessel up and down and side to side for around 1 minute. This oxygenates the yeast, which gets it to wake up and start working on the beer. Once you're done shaking the vessel, attach the airlock to the silicone stopper and fill the lock with a little diluted disinfectant or just ordinary water. Put the stopper in the fermentation vessel.

You need to put the vessel somewhere dark, usually at room temperature (18–22°C/64–72°F). Some beers need to ferment at warmer or colder temperatures, so check each recipe. Then the 2-week wait begins. This is how long it takes for the yeast to form alcohol in your beer. As a rule, the most aggressive phase of the fermentation process takes places in the first 36 hours. Foam and bubbles will form in the airlock during this time. Then it may feel like everything has stopped, but if you look closely you'll see that there is a bubble in the airlock every minute or so. When it has completely stopped bubbling in the airlock, the fermentation process is complete and it's time to bottle.

Pour the wort from the saucepan into the fermentation vessel.

Activate the yeast by shaking the vessel.

WAIT
2 W

Tip
Buy a few beers. They'll taste good and you can hang onto the glass bottles for bottling your own beer.

FOR

EKS

7. Bottling

Now it'll really feel like you have your own mini-brewery. When you put the first cap on a bottle filled with your beer, it's impossible not to feel a real sense of pride. It's almost done! Just 2 weeks left to allow the carbonic acid to build up inside the bottle. Then your beers will be ready!

1. Make a primer

A primer is quite simply a layer of sugar. Thanks to this, carbonic acid forms in the beer. Pour 100 ml (3½ fl oz/ scant ½ cup) water into the small saucepan and set over the highest heat. Add 2 tablespoons caster (superfine) sugar. Bring to the boil so that the sugar dissolves. Allow the sugar mixture to cool to room temperature.

2. Disinfect

You need to disinfect everything that comes into contact with the beer. Fill a 10-litre (21-pint) bucket with water and add the correct amount of disinfectant. Disinfect all equipment: the siphon, bottle caps, bottle capper and even the big saucepan and all the bottles that are to be used. It's normally sufficient to dip the bottles one by one into the bucket, leave them there for a few seconds and then remove them. It's fine to use bottles that you have already drunk from, just ensure that they have been cleaned before you disinfect them. Once everything is disinfected and the primer is ready, you can get on with bottling.

3. Bottling

Put the fermentation vessel on a stable surface, such as your kitchen work surface (it's worth putting a damp tea (dish) towel under the vessel to help keep it steady). Put the 5-litre (10½-pint) saucepan on a stool in front of the kitchen counter to create a height difference between the vessel and saucepan. Remove the silicone stopper from the fermentation vessel. Put the siphon into the vessel just above the yeast cake that has formed at the bottom of the vessel. Blow air into the siphon to create pressure. When the beer begins to run through the siphon, fill the saucepan with beer. Avoid the yeast cake at the bottom of the fermentation vessel. If you added hops or flavouring straight into the vessel during fermentation, you will also need to filter the beer using a strainer, placed on top of the saucepan. Once the saucepan

You will need:
Brewing equipment

siphon

disinfectant

bottle capper

bottle caps

about 12 bottles

Kitchen equipment

1 large saucepan, minimum 5 litres (10½ pints)

1 small saucepan

10-litre (21-pint) bucket

Ingredients

2 tablespoons caster (superfine) sugar

A height difference is required for the siphon to work.

is filled with beer, remove the siphon and disinfect it again. Put the saucepan on the work surface, preferably with a damp tea towel underneath to keep it stable. Once the primer is at room temperature, stir it into the saucepan filled with beer. Put your bottles beneath the saucepan – for example, on the stool you were previously using for the saucepan. Put the siphon into the saucepan and create pressure using your mouth. Once the beer is running through the siphon, you should quickly put it into one of the bottles and fill it with beer, leaving 1–2 cm (½–¾ in) of air at the top of the bottle neck. Continue to fill the rest of the bottles. If you have a hose clip for your siphon, use this to stop the flow as you move from bottle to bottle; otherwise it's fine to pinch the siphon using your fingers.

4. Capping and releasing carbonic acid
Once all the bottles are filled, you need to add bottle caps, ensuring that all the bottle caps are disinfected. Put a cap on a filled bottle and use your bottle capper to seal, then store the bottles in a dark place at room temperature. After 2 weeks, the beer will be ready to drink, once the small quantity of yeast still in it has consumed the sugar from the primer and transformed it into carbonic acid.

Six prejudices about brewing beer

1. It smells
Kitchen brewing is odour-free. Since you are brewing a smaller volume, no odours are formed.

2. It's difficult
It's no more difficult than baking bread.

3. It gives you a stomach ache
That was back when beer was brewed with additives. Nowadays, we brew using exactly the same raw ingredients as microbreweries – it's completely risk free.

4. It's not like real beer
But. Well. It looks like beer. It smells like beer. It tastes like beer. It IS beer.

5. It takes up lots of space
All you need is space for the fermentation vessel and 12 to 14 beer bottles. Kitchen brewing is optimised for a completely normal kitchen.

6. It's banned
No. As long as you or your friends drink the beer, it's fine.

BEER SCHOOL

Right, here are five beer school tests you can study for and add to your CV. The first lesson at every beer school is to learn the difference between lager and ale. These two styles divide the world into two camps. The camp that loves classic German beer (lager) and the one that seeks out a slightly more challenging beer (ale). Once you've got the hang of these two styles, and tasted your way through a few different lagers and ales, you'll soon realise that the two opposing sides ought to make peace.

Lager vs. ale

In pure taste terms, naturally there are differences between lager and ale, but the big differences are in terms of brewing technique. It's all a matter of over-fermented and under-fermented beer. Lager is under-fermented, which means it ferments at lower temperatures (8–15°C/46–59°F). Ale is over-fermented, and ferments best at room temperature (around 18–22°C/64–71°F). Ale is good for kitchen brewing, since it is easier to ferment at room temperature. Another reason why one typically chooses to kitchen brew ale is that flavour flaws don't occur as easily in an ale as they do in a lager.

There are an awful lot of beer styles and types in the ale and lager families. Here are the most important ones (in our view):

India Pale Ale (IPA) The story goes that the British couldn't bear to be without their ale when they colonised India. To make sure that the beer kept all the way to India, they went heavy on the hops (which act as a preservative), which resulted in high bitterness, high alcohol content and lots of flavour. Nowadays, every microbrewery out there makes their own IPA. The colour should be amber to be in keeping with the style.

American Pale Ale (APA) This is the little brother (or sister) of the IPA. It's a milder version of IPA, is often a little paler, has a little less alcohol and doesn't contain as much hops – making it less bitter. Just because it's called American doesn't mean it has to be made in the USA. Like the IPA, a multitude of versions are made around the world.

Pilsner A typical lager. This is a beer with a relatively high amount of bitterness and with the flavour and aroma of grass and other herbal tones. In terms of colour, it's light and it should be clear in consistency.

Wheat beer Wheat beer is ale, but at the light end of the scale. It is brewed (mostly) using wheat malt instead of barley malt. Using wheat malt means you end up with more foam in the beer. In terms of flavour, wheat beers can vary a lot, ranging from banana to lemon flavour. If you think that wheat beer seems fresh, then you're not far wrong. This is because there should be lots of carbonic acid in the beer, which results in a more joyous and effervescent mouth feel.

Stout and porter Contain hard roasted malt, which gives the beers a dark colour. Often, you let the malt take up more space than the hops, which means that stout and porter taste breadier, roasted and with tones of coffee or chocolate. Also, the more malt you add, the more alcohol you end up with, since more malt means more sugar for the yeast to ferment.

Saison *'Saison'* is the French for 'season'. Originally, it was a Belgian beer brewed for seasonal workers in the fields during the summer. It wasn't all that important what got added to the mash or the hops, they just used whatever they had. Not much has changed. In the flavouring for a saison today, you'll find far more than just hops, including things like lemon balm, raspberry, gooseberries and much more. Saison benefits from fermenting at a slightly higher temperature to give the beer a peppery taste.

Beer styles

1. Pilsner
2. Wheat beer
3. Saison
4. American Pale Ale
5. India Pale Ale
6. Stout and porter

1. **2.** **3.**

4.

5.

6.

THE RECIPES

Just like chefs, we kitchen brewers like to follow the seasons. Depending on the time of year, nature offers plenty of options when it comes to what you can use in your brew. Rhubarb in early summer is great for seasoning wheat beer, while autumn berries and fruit are the perfect addition to an IPA.

The different seasons also influence what you want to drink. In spring, you want something fresh, in the summer you want something cool, and autumn is the harvest season and the time for cider. Once we stumble into winter, we want our beer like the days – dark. For this reason, we have opted to divide our recipes into four categories based on the four seasons.

Important information about the recipes

- *All hops measurements are based on hop pellets rather than hop cones.*
- *All malt measurements are based on crushed malt, not whole malt.*
- *Read the basic method (see pages 20–31) before starting, as you'll find detailed instructions there for each step of the brewing process.*

Normal brewing recipes use grams as their unit of measurement. We've chosen to use volume for those ingredients you have to measure yourself. We know most people have volume measures at home, but not everyone has a set of scales. We want to help you to start brewing, which means we think it's more important to make brewing easy than to have the weight right down to the last gram.

1 teaspoon of hops is roughly the equivalent of 5 g (⅛ oz)
200 ml (7 fl oz/scant 1 cup) malt is approximately 100 g (3½ oz)
1 packet of dried yeast weighs 10–11.5 g (¼ oz)

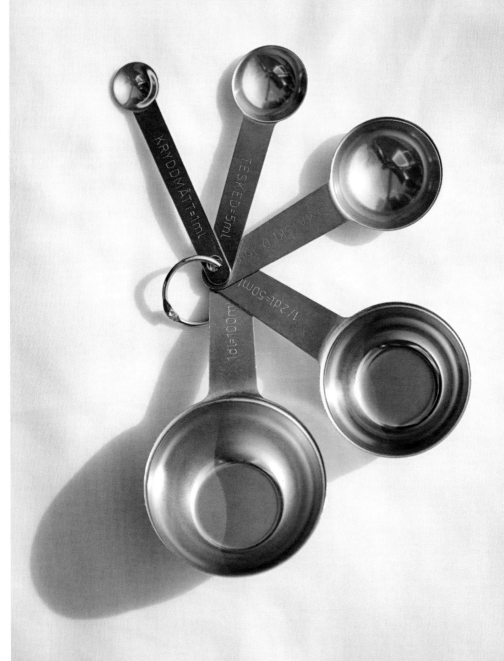

Spring Brewing

A saison, an Easter beer, a very modern lager, a crispy wheat beer and a Swedish folköl.

CORIANDER SAISON

The saison is the beer of leftovers – throw in anything you can find in the larder. The base is a pale Belgian beer, normally flavoured with coriander (cilantro), chilli, raspberry or other herbs, berries and fruits. This recipe provides a drinkable beer a high degree of guzzlability. It is refreshing, with a hint of pepper and an aroma of coriander.

Day 1 – Mash, separate and boil
Heat 1.7 litres (4 pints) of water to 68°C (154°F). Stir in the wheat malt and CaraAmber. Take the saucepan off the heat, put the lid on and leave to stand for about 15 minutes. Separate out the malt (see page 25).

Add cold water to bring the total volume of liquid in the pan to 4.5 litres (10 pints). Set over the highest heat and add the spraymalt. Stir until all the lumps are gone. Boil for 25 minutes, then carefully stir in the hops. Continue to boil for a further 5 minutes, then leave to cool in the saucepan (see page 26).

Once the wort has cooled to 20°C (68°F), transfer it to the fermentation vessel using a disinfected strainer and funnel. Add the yeast to the vessel and shake. Attach the fermentation lock to the silicone stopper, fill the airlock and push the stopper into the vessel. The yeast temperature should be 18–30°C (64–86°F). This beer benefits from being fermented warm to increase the pepperiness. One tip is to position the fermentation vessel near to a radiator (but it mustn't get warmer than 30°C/86°F).

Day 11 – Flavouring
Disinfect your hands, gently remove the silicone stopper and add the coriander to the vessel. Replace the stopper.

Day 14 – Bottling
Prepare a primer and follow the bottling instructions (see page 30). The beer will be ready to drink after another 14 days.

Facts
Style: Saison
Bitterness: Very low
Goes with: When you need something refreshing
Alcohol content: 5.5%

Ingredients
Malt
200 ml (7 fl oz/scant 1 cup) wheat malt
200 ml (7 fl oz/scant 1 cup) CaraAmber
500 g (1 lb 2 oz) spraymalt

Hops
4 tablespoons Citra

Yeast
½ packet of Lallemand Belle Saison

Flavouring
1 bunch of coriander (cilantro), rinsed and chopped

Primer
100 ml (3½ fl oz/scant ½ cup) water
2 tablespoons caster (superfine) sugar

EASTER BEER

At Easter, you want to drink a beer that complements as many different flavours as possible, since we come across Easter dishes that may be sweet, rich or salty. The beer should simply taste good, rather than standing out too much. It should be cold, it should be fairly light and, if you ask us, it should also be quite dry. This recipe is a golden ale, first conceived of by the British when competition from foreign pale lagers really began to heat up. A good golden ale should contain pale malt and allow the bitterness of the hops to be expressed just enough.

Day 1 – Mash, separate and boil
In a saucepan, heat 1.7 litres (4 pints) of water to 68°C (154°F). Stir in the pale ale malt and CaraAmber. Take the saucepan off the heat, put the lid on and leave to stand for about 15 minutes. Separate out the malt (see page 25).

Add cold water to bring the total volume of liquid in the pan to 4.5 litres (10 pints). Set over the highest heat and add the spraymalt. Stir until all the lumps are gone. Bring to the boil, then carefully add 1 tablespoon East Kent Golding and 1 tablespoon Fuggle. Continue to boil and, after 15 minutes, add a further 1 tablespoon East Kent Golding and 1 tablespoon Fuggle. Boil for a further 15 minutes, then leave to cool in the saucepan (see page 26).

Once the wort has cooled to 20°C (68°F), transfer it to the fermentation vessel using a strainer and funnel. Ensure that all equipment is disinfected. Add the yeast to the fermentation vessel and shake. Attach the fermentation lock to the silicone stopper, fill the airlock and push the stopper into the vessel. The yeast temperature should be maintained at 15–24°C (59–75°F).

Day 14 – Bottling
Prepare a primer and follow the bottling instructions (see page 30). The beer will be ready to drink after another 14 days.

Facts
Style: Golden ale
Bitterness: Just right
Goes with: Easter Sunday lunch
Alcohol content: 6%

Ingredients
Malt
400 ml (13 fl oz/1½ cups) pale ale malt
400 ml (13 fl oz/1½ cups) CaraAmber
500 g (1 lb 2 oz) spraymalt

Hops
2 tablespoons East Kent Golding
2 tablespoons Fuggle

Yeast
½ packet of Fermentis S-04

Primer
100 ml (3½ fl oz/scant ½ cup) water
2 tablespoons caster (superfine) sugar

MODERN LAGER

Recipes – Spring

Sharp, crispy and hoppy – that's how to describe a modern lager. A beer for when you're after a flavourful craft beer, but don't want to drink yet another IPA. This recipe makes a pleasingly hoppy lager with a hint of grapefruit and citrus. Lager yeast generally needs to be at a lower temperature during fermentation than ale yeasts do. That's why this is a good beer to brew as spring approaches and the temperature outdoors is between 8–15°C (46–59°F), which means you can ferment the beer in cool conditions in a cellar, garage or shed. Just make sure your fermentation vessel isn't exposed to sunlight, or at risk of being stolen by the neighbours!

Day 1 – Mash, separate and boil

In a saucepan, heat 1.7 litres (4 pints) of water to 70°C (158°F). Stir in the pilsner malt and CaraMalt. Take the saucepan off the heat, put the lid on and leave to stand for about 15 minutes. Separate out the malt (see page 25).

Add cold water to bring the total volume of liquid in a pan to 4.5 litres (10 pints). Set over the highest heat and add the spraymalt. Stir until all the lumps are gone. Bring to the boil, then carefully add 2 tablespoons Chinook and 2 tablespoons Cascade. Boil for 27 minutes, then add a further 2 tablespoons Chinook and 2 tablespoons Cascade. Boil for a further 3 minutes, then leave to cool in the saucepan (see page 26).

Once the wort has cooled to 20°C (68°F), transfer it to the fermentation vessel using a strainer and funnel. Ensure that all equipment is disinfected. Add the yeast to the fermentation vessel and shake. Attach the fermentation lock to the silicone stopper, fill the airlock and push the stopper into the vessel. The yeast temperature should be maintained at 9–15°C (48–59°F).

Day 14 – Bottling

Prepare a primer and follow the bottling instructions (see page 30). The beer will be ready to drink after another 14 days.

Facts

Style: Modern lager

Bitterness: Just right

Goes with: Hanging out with friends

Alcohol content: 5%

Ingredients

Malt

200 ml (7 fl oz/scant 1 cup) pilsner malt

200 ml (7 fl oz/scant 1 cup) CaraMalt

500 g (1 lb 2 oz) spraymalt

Hops

4 tablespoons Chinook

4 tablespoons Cascade

Yeast

½ packet of Fermentis S-23

Primer

100 ml (3½ fl oz/scant ½ cup) water

2 tablespoons caster (superfine) sugar

WHEAT BEER

Recipes – Spring

Wheat beer often splits beer drinkers down the middle. Many love it, while others simply cannot grasp why it should ever be put into a beer glass. We're amongst the former. The fun thing about brewing wheat beer is that you get to experience developing proper foam on a home-brewed beer. The wheat means that the foam is a little thicker than usual. This is a classic wheat beer using a Czech hop known as Saaz.

Day 1 – Mash, separate and boil
In a large saucepan, heat 1.7 litres (4 pints) of water to 68°C (154°F). Stir in the wheat malt. Take the saucepan off the heat, put the lid on and leave to stand for about 15 minutes. Separate out the malt (see page 25).

Add cold water to bring the total volume of liquid in a pan to 5 litres (10½ pints). Set over the highest heat and add the spraymalt. Stir until all the lumps are gone. Bring to the boil, then carefully add 1 tablespoon Saaz. Boil for 50 minutes and then add the orange zest. Continue to boil for 10 minutes. Add a further 2 tablespoons Saaz, then leave to cool in the saucepan (see page 26).

Once the wort has cooled to 20°C (68°F), transfer it to the fermentation vessel using a strainer and funnel. Ensure that all equipment is disinfected. Add the yeast to the fermentation vessel and shake. Attach the fermentation lock to the silicone stopper, fill the airlock and push the stopper into the vessel. The yeast temperature should be maintained at 18–30°C (64–86°F).

Day 14 – Bottling
Prepare a primer and follow the bottling instructions (see page 30). The beer will be ready to drink after another 14 days.

Facts
Style: Witbier
Bitterness: Just right
Goes with: A picnic
Alcohol content: 5%

Ingredients
Malt
200 ml (7 fl oz/scant 1 cup)
   wheat malt
500 g (1 lb 2 oz) spraymalt

Hops
3 tablespoons Saaz

Flavouring
zest of 1 orange

Yeast
½ packet of Bavarian Wheat
   (Mangrove Jack's M20)

Primer
100 ml (3½ fl oz/scant ½ cup)
   water
2 tablespoons caster (superfine)
   sugar

FOLKÖL

Recipes – Spring

Folköl is every Swedish beer lover's guilty pleasure. It's a Swedish icon that has a maximum alcohol strength of 3.5% and so can be sold in supermarkets rather than via the state monopoly. And you can make it even better through kitchen brewing (by adding more hops!).

Day 1 – Mash, separate and boil
In a large saucepan, heat 1.7 litres (4 pints) of water to 68°C (154°F). Stir in the CaraAroma. Take the saucepan off the heat, put the lid on and leave to stand for about 15 minutes. Separate out the malt (see page 25).

Add cold water to bring the total volume of liquid in the pan to 5 litres (10½ pints). Set over the highest heat and add the spraymalt. Stir until all the lumps are gone. Boil for 10 minutes, then carefully stir in the hops. Continue to boil for a further 5 minutes, then leave to cool in the saucepan (see page 26).

Once the wort has cooled to 20°C (68°F), transfer it to the fermentation vessel using a strainer and funnel. Ensure that all equipment is disinfected. Add the yeast to the fermentation vessel and shake. Attach the fermentation lock to the silicone stopper, fill the airlock and push the stopper into the vessel. The yeast temperature should be maintained at 15–24°C (59–75°F).

Day 14 – Bottling
Prepare a primer and follow the bottling instructions (see page 30). The beer will be ready to drink after another 14 days.

Facts

Style: India Pale Ale
Bitterness: Just right
Goes with: Watching sports
Alcohol content: 3.5%

Ingredients

Malt
200 ml (7 fl oz/scant 1 cup)
  CaraAroma
500 g (1 lb 2 oz) spraymalt

Hops
5 tablespoons Centennial

Yeast
½ packet of Fermentis US-05

Primer
100 ml (3½ fl oz/scant ½ cup)
  water
2 tablespoons caster (superfine)
  sugar

How long will the beer keep?

Your kitchen-brewed beer will be at its very best
3–4 weeks after being bottled. It will continue
to taste good for at least 6 months, but since hops
are a fresh product, the beer will start to lose its
flavour. The beer will never go bad or be in any way
hazardous, but it won't taste as good after 1 year.

Summer Brewing

*A low-alcohol lättöl, a BBQ beer,
a break beer, a coffee beer
and a refreshing hop juice.*

LOW-ALCOHOL LÄTTÖL

Recipes – Summer

For many people, long summer days means it's time for a party. Food, beer, wine ... maybe a few more beers as the day goes on. In short, there's often a lot of alcohol at a summer party. Probably too much for many. That's why we recommend a good lättöl, a very low-alcohol Swedish beer, which can either be the only thing you drink, or a smart beverage to partner up with the stronger drinks.

Day 1 – Mash, separate and boil

In a large saucepan, heat 1.7 litres (4 pints) of water to 68°C (154°F). Stir in the CaraRed and pilsner malt. Take the saucepan off the heat, put the lid on and leave to stand for about 15 minutes. Separate out the malt (see page 25).

Add cold water to bring the total volume of liquid in the pan to 4.5 litres (10 pints). Set over the highest heat. Bring to the boil, then carefully add the hops and boil for 15 minutes, then leave to cool in the saucepan (see page 26).

Once the wort has cooled to 20°C (68°F), transfer it to the fermentation vessel using a strainer and funnel. Ensure that all equipment is disinfected. Add the yeast to the fermentation vessel and shake. Attach the fermentation lock to the silicone stopper, fill the airlock and push the stopper into the vessel. The yeast temperature should be maintained at 15–24°C (59–75°F).

Day 14 – Bottling

Prepare a primer and follow the bottling instructions (see page 30). The beer will be ready to drink after another 14 days.

Facts

Style: Lättöl

Bitterness: Low

Goes with: A family party

Alcohol content: 1.5%

Ingredients

Malt

400 ml (13 fl oz/1½ cups) CaraRed

400 ml (13 fl oz/1½ cups) pilsner malt

Hops

2 tablespoons Amarillo

Yeast

½ packet of Fermentis S-04

Primer

100 ml (3½ fl oz/scant ½ cup) water

2 tablespoons caster (superfine) sugar

AMERICAN BEER-B-Q

Recipes – Summer

Yes, beer goes well with barbecued food, but isn't it even better when you drink beer while barbecuing? The best kind is a fresh beer you can drink straight from the bottle. For barbecues, we prefer an American Pale Ale, a fairly dry beer with plenty of flavour that borders on fruity. The reason for it being American is because hops from the USA are used, which are almost always fruitier than hops from Europe.

Day 1 – Mash, separate and boil
In a large saucepan, heat 1.7 litres (4 pints) of water to 68°C (154°F). Stir in the crystal malt. Take the saucepan off the heat, put the lid on and leave to stand for about 15 minutes. Separate out the malt (see page 25).

Add cold water to bring the total volume of liquid in a pan to 4.5 litres (10 pints). Set over the highest heat and add the spraymalt. Stir until all the lumps are gone. Boil for 5 minutes, then carefully stir in the hops. Continue to boil for a further 10 minutes, then leave to cool in the saucepan (see page 26).

Once the wort has cooled to 20°C (68°F), transfer it to the fermentation vessel using a strainer and funnel. Ensure that all equipment is disinfected. Add the yeast to the fermentation vessel and shake. Attach the fermentation lock to the silicone stopper, fill the airlock and push the stopper into the vessel. The yeast temperature should be maintained at 15–24°C (59–75°F).

Day 14 – Bottling
Prepare a primer and follow the bottling instructions (see page 30). The beer will be ready to drink after another 14 days.

Facts
Style: American Pale Ale
Bitterness: Just right
Goes with: A barbecue
Alcohol content: 6%

Ingredients
Malt
400 ml (13 fl oz/1½ cups) crystal malt
500 g (1 lb 2 oz) spraymalt

Hops
5 tablespoons Citra

Yeast
½ packet of Fermentis US-05

Primer
100 ml (3½ fl oz/scant ½ cup) water
2 tablespoons caster (superfine) sugar

BREAK BEER

Recipes – Summer

It goes without saying that a large glass of water is a great thirst quencher after hard labour in the summer heat. But some jobs, like mowing the lawn, just seem to slip by quicker if you know there's a cold beer waiting for you at the end. The kind of cold beer that stings your mouth with all of its spiky carbonation. Our perfect mowing beer is a session IPA, with a lower alcohol content of around 4 per cent, but still with everything you love about IPA – bitterness and fruity tones.

Day 1 – Mash, separate and boil
In a large saucepan, heat 1.7 litres (4 pints) of water to 68°C (154°F). Stir in the CaraRed. Take the saucepan off the heat, put the lid on and leave to stand for about 15 minutes. Separate out the malt (see page 25).

Add cold water to bring the total volume of liquid in the pan to 4.5 litres (10 pints). Set over the highest heat and add the spraymalt. Stir until all the lumps are gone. Bring to the boil, then carefully add 2 tablespoons Chinook. Continue to boil for 27 minutes, then add 1 tablespoon Chinook and 1 tablespoon Citra. Leave to boil for a further 3 minutes, then leave to cool in the saucepan (see page 26).

Once the wort has cooled to 20°C (68°F), transfer it to the fermentation vessel using a strainer and funnel. Ensure that all equipment is disinfected. Add the yeast to the fermentation vessel and shake. Attach the fermentation lock to the silicone stopper, fill the airlock and push the stopper into the vessel. The yeast temperature should be maintained be 15–24°C (59–75°F).

Day 11 – Dry hopping
Disinfect your hands, gently remove the silicone stopper and add 2 tablespoons Citra to the vessel. Replace the stopper.

Day 14 – Bottling
Prepare a primer and follow the bottling instructions (see page 30). The beer will be ready to drink after another 14 days.

Facts
Style: Session IPA
Bitterness: High
Goes with: Recovery
Alcohol content: 4%

Ingredients
Malt
100 ml (3½ fl oz/scant ½ cup) CaraRed
500 g (1 lb 2 oz) spraymalt

Hops
3 tablespoons Chinook
3 tablespoons Citra

Yeast
½ packet of Fermentis S-04

Primer
100 ml (3½ fl oz/scant ½ cup) water
2 tablespoons caster (superfine) sugar

COFFEE PORTER

Recipes – Summer

Many people associate porters solely with autumn and winter. We've never understood why. Of course you can drink a dark beer in the summer too! And it's even more fun if you liven up your coffee break with a coffee porter. To bring out the coffee tones in the beer, you can choose to use malts that, when heated, give off flavours reminiscent of coffee, or you can emphasise the coffee flavour even more with a shot of black filter coffee added during fermentation. It's as simple as that.

Day 1 – Mash, separate and boil
In a large saucepan, heat 1.7 litres (4 pints) of water to 68°C (154°F). Stir in the roasted barley and Carafa II. Take the saucepan off the heat, put the lid on and leave to stand for about 15 minutes. Separate out the malt (see page 25).

Add cold water to bring the total volume of liquid in the pan to 5 litres (10½ pints). Set over the highest heat and add the spraymalt. Stir until all the lumps are gone. Bring to the boil, then carefully add the hops. Leave to boil for a further 1 hour, then cool in the saucepan (see page 26).

Once the wort has cooled to 20°C (68°F), transfer it to the fermentation vessel using a strainer and funnel. Ensure that all equipment is disinfected. Add the yeast to the fermentation vessel and shake. Attach the fermentation lock to the silicone stopper, fill the airlock and push the stopper into the vessel. The yeast temperature should be maintained at 15–24°C (59–75°F).

Day 11 – Flavouring
Disinfect your hands, gently remove the silicone stopper and add 4–5 tablespoons freshly brewed, cooled filter coffee to the vessel. Replace the stopper.

Day 14 – Bottling
Prepare a primer and follow the bottling instructions (see page 30). The beer will be ready to drink after another 14 days.

Facts
Style: Coffee porter
Bitterness: Low
Goes with: Coffee and cake
Alcohol content: 5.5%

Ingredients
Malt
100 ml (3½ fl oz/scant ½ cup) roasted barley
50 ml (2 fl oz/¼ cup) Carafa II
500 g (1 lb 2 oz) spraymalt

Hops
2 tablespoons Saaz

Yeast
½ packet of Fermentis US-05

Flavouring
4–5 tablespoons freshly brewed filter coffee

Primer
100 ml (3½ fl oz/scant ½ cup) water
2 tablespoons caster (superfine) sugar

HOP JUICE

Yes, you read that right. Beer in the form of juice. This IPA is silky smooth, not too bitter and bursting with fruity hops. A good hop juice is like a juicy, refreshing mango juice. It is an abundance of American hops (some preferably added at the end of boiling) that have this effect. And don't forget that a genuine New England IPA should be cloudy. You shouldn't be able to see through it. That means it's good. Really good.

Day 1 – Mash, separate and boil
Heat 1.7 litres (4 pints) of water to 68°C (154°F). Stir in the rolled oats, puffed wheat and pale ale malt. Take the saucepan off the heat, put the lid on and leave to stand for about 15 minutes. Separate out the malt (see page 25).

Add cold water to bring the total volume of liquid in the pan to 4.5 litres (10 pints). Set over the highest heat and add the spraymalt. Stir until all the lumps are gone. Bring to the boil, then carefully add 1½ tablespoons Mosaic and boil for a further 27 minutes. Add 1½ tablespoons Nelson Sauvin and 1½ tablespoons Citra. Boil for a further 3 minutes, then add a further 1½ tablespoons Mosaic and leave to cool in the saucepan (see page 26).

Once the wort has cooled to 20°C (68°F), transfer it to the fermentation vessel using a strainer and funnel. Ensure that all equipment is disinfected. Add the yeast to the fermentation vessel and shake. Attach the fermentation lock to the silicone stopper, fill the airlock and push the stopper into the vessel. The yeast temperature should be maintained at 15–24°C (59–75°F).

Day 11 – Dry hopping
Disinfect your hands, gently remove the silicone stopper and add 1 tablespoon Nelson Sauvin, 1 tablespoon Mosaic and 1 tablespoon Citra to the vessel. Replace the stopper.

Day 14 – Bottling
Prepare a primer and follow the bottling instructions (see page 30). The beer will be ready to drink after another 14 days.

Facts
Style: New England IPA
Bitterness: Just right
Goes with: A good friend
Alcohol content: 5.5%

Ingredients
Malt
200 ml (7 fl oz/scant 1 cup) rolled (old fashioned) oats
200 ml (7 fl oz/scant 1 cup) puffed wheat
200 ml (7 fl oz/scant 1 cup) pale ale malt
500 g (1 lb 2 oz) spraymalt

Hops
4 tablespoons Mosaic
2½ tablespoons Nelson Sauvin
2½ tablespoons Citra

Yeast
½ packet of Fermentis S-04

Primer
100 ml (3½ fl oz/scant ½ cup) water
2 tablespoons caster (superfine) sugar

Autumn (Fall) Brewing

An apple cider, a double IPA,
a harvest beer, something
delicious for Oktoberfest
and a steam beer.

You will need:
Brewing equipment

fermentation vessel
fermentation lock
silicone stopper
disinfectant
ingredients

Making cider

The basic method for making cider is to take apple juice and let it ferment. The yeast forms alcohol from the sugar in the apple juice. Traditionally, you don't add yeast but simply let the bacteria on the apples act as yeast, which allows the apple juice to ferment and form cider.

Cider can be varied by mixing different types of apples and using different types of yeast. The longer you leave cider to ferment, the stronger it is in terms of alcohol and the drier it gets, as the sugar is turned into alcohol and leaves more space for the harsher acidity. The more types of apples you mix into the apple juice, the juicier and more complex the flavour becomes, which can add acidity, sweetness and bitterness.

Some may find homemade cider to be very, very dry. This is because the apples only contain simple sugars, which means that the sugar is entirely fermented. Some people like this, while others may want to sweeten the cider a little. There are a few options for making cider sweeter, such as using tablets to stop the yeast fermenting, and adding more sugar to the apple juice. However, the easiest way is to pour a little less cider into the glass when serving and to dilute it with sweet apple juice. Simple and delicious!

Good cider apples

It's fine to make cider using common garden apples. There is a wide variety of apples available ranging from acidic to sweet and both types are good for cider making.

APPLE CIDER

Recipes – Autumn (Fall)

In parallel with all the microbreweries that have appeared in recent years, the number of cider presses has also increased. At many of these, you can even bring your own apples to press. The apples from an average apple tree usually produce around 30 litres (65 pints) of juice. For your own cider, all you need is freshly pressed apple juice and yeast. In practice, you can use more or less any ale yeast, but in this recipe we've chosen a specially developed cider yeast. The result is a dry cider.

You can make a great aperitif using cider. Mix cider and cava (or any other sparkling wine) 50/50 in a Champagne glass. Drink and enjoy!

Day 1 – Fermenting

Making cider is a lot easier than brewing beer (see page 71). All you have to do is thoroughly disinfect the fermentation vessel, pour the apple juice into it and then add the yeast. Seal the vessel with the silicone stopper and airlock, just as you would when brewing beer. Leave the juice to ferment for 2–4 weeks in the vessel. The yeast temperature should be maintained at 12–28°C (54–82°F).

Day 14/28 – Bottling

Bottle the cider in the same way you do when brewing beer, including the primer (see page 30). The longer you wait to drink the cider after bottling, the better it will taste. We find that giving it around 8 months results in the best outcome. However, you should consume the cider within 12 months to make sure it doesn't go off.

Facts

Style: Dry cider

Sweetness: Well, it's a little more reserved...

Goes with: Appetisers when drunk as an aperitif

Alcohol content: 4–5% (depending on the sweetness of your juice)

Ingredients

Juice

4–5 litres (8½–10½ pints) apple juice

Yeast

1 packet of Mangrove Jack's M02

Primer

100 ml (3½ fl oz/scant ½ cup) water

2 tablespoons caster (superfine) sugar

DOUBLE IPA

Just as the casseroles start to emerge and the beef bourguignon is simmering away on the stove, it's time to drink a double IPA or, as it is also known, an Imperial IPA. Double is in the name because it tastes twice as good, but is also twice as strong. This is the 4×4 of the beer world. It has everything you love about an ordinary IPA (car), but everything has been enhanced (higher clearance, four-wheel drive). A dubious, even faltering simile, but nevertheless, double IPA has more bitterness, a little more fruitiness and a little more strength. In short, a little bit more deliciousness.

Day 1 – Mash, separate and boil
In a large saucepan, heat 1.7 litres (4 pints) of water to 70°C (158°F). Stir in the CaraRed, wheat malt and rolled oats. Take the saucepan off the heat, put the lid on and leave to stand for about 15 minutes. Separate out the malt (see page 25).

Add cold water to bring the total volume of liquid to 5 litres (10½ pints). Set over the highest heat and add the spraymalt. Stir until all the lumps are gone. Bring to the boil, then carefully add 1 tablespoon Simcoe. Boil for 40 minutes and then add 1 tablespoon Centennial. Continue to boil for 20 minutes. Add a further 1 tablespoon Centennial and 1 tablespoon Simcoe, then leave to cool in the saucepan (see page 26).

Once the wort has cooled to 20°C (68°F), transfer it to the fermentation vessel using a strainer and funnel. Ensure that all equipment is disinfected. Add the yeast to the fermentation vessel and shake. Attach the fermentation lock to the silicone stopper, fill the airlock and push the stopper into the vessel. The yeast temperature should be maintained at 15–24°C (59–75°F).

Day 11 – Dry hopping
Disinfect your hands, gently remove the silicone stopper and add 2 tablespoons Simcoe to the vessel. Replace the silicone stopper.

Day 14 – Bottling
Prepare a primer and follow the bottling instructions (see page 30). The beer will be ready to drink after another 14 days.

Facts
Style: Imperial IPA
Bitterness: High
Goes with: Casseroles
Alcohol content: 7–8%

Ingredients
Malt
200 ml (7 fl oz/scant 1 cup) CaraRed
200 ml (7 fl oz/scant 1 cup) wheat malt
200 ml (7 fl oz/scant 1 cup) rolled (old fashioned) oats
1 kg (2 lb 3 oz) spraymalt

Hops
4 tablespoons Simcoe
2 tablespoons Centennial

Yeast
1 packet of Fermentis US-05

Primer
100 ml (3½ fl oz/scant ½ cup) water
2 tablespoons caster (superfine) sugar

HARVEST BEER

Recipes – Autumn (Fall)

In late August, the gardens and shops are usually filled with beautiful fruits and berries. Currants and raspberries are great ways to flavour your beer. In this recipe, we've chosen raspberries, but you can use the same quantity of blackcurrants or redcurrants. To achieve the right raspberry feel, we only use light malt, which allows the berries to give the beer its colour. This beer that it tastes best when fresh – it won't improve if matured, but will simply lose the berry flavour as time passes. So make sure you enjoy it while it's fresh.

Day 1 – Mash, separate and boil
In a large saucepan, heat 1.7 litres (4 pints) of water to 72°C (162°F). Stir in the wheat malt. Take the saucepan off the heat, put the lid on and leave to stand for about 15 minutes. Separate out the malt (see page 25).

Add cold water to bring the total volume of liquid in the pan to 4.5 litres (10 pints). Set over the highest heat and add the spraymalt. Stir until all the lumps are gone. Boil for 15 minutes, then carefully add the hops and leave to cool in the saucepan (see page 26).

Once the wort has cooled to 20°C (68°F), transfer it to the fermentation vessel using a strainer and funnel. Ensure that all equipment is disinfected. Add the yeast to the fermentation vessel and shake. Attach the fermentation lock to the silicone stopper, fill the airlock and push the stopper into the vessel. The yeast temperature should be maintained at 18–30°C (64–86°F).

Day 11 – Flavouring
Pasteurise the raspberries by boiling them in a saucepan. Allow to cool. Disinfect your hands, carefully remove the silicone stopper and pour the pasteurised raspberries into the vessel before replacing the stopper.

Day 14 – Bottling
Prepare a primer and follow the bottling instructions (see page 30). It may be worth filtering the beer when transferring it from the fermentation vessel to the saucepan to remove the raspberry seeds. The beer will be ready to drink after another 14 days.

Facts
Style: Raspberry wheat
Bitterness: Weak
Goes with: Starters
Alcohol content: 4–5% (depending on how sweet your berries are)

Ingredients
Malt
200 ml (7 fl oz/scant 1 cup) wheat malt
500 g (1 lb 2 oz) spraymalt

Hops
2 tablespoons Hallertau

Yeast
½ packet of Bavarian Wheat (Mangrove Jack's M20)

Flavouring
200–300 g (7–10½ oz) fresh raspberries

Primer
100 ml (3½ fl oz/scant ½ cup) water
2 tablespoons caster (superfine) sugar

OKTOBERFEST

Recipes – Autumn (Fall)

The only thing about the German phenomenon of Oktoberfest that is really of any interest is the beer. Although there's nothing wrong with a bit of oompah-oompah music, for a while anyway, there's nothing like a good Oktober beer – a classic German lager. Because it's delicious! The beer is just the right level of bitter, and the hops feature earthier tones of pine needles compared with fruity American hops. The colour is relatively pale, almost golden. Remember that the beer needs to be cold-fermented.

Day 1 – Mash, separate and boil
In a large saucepan, heat 1.7 litres (4 pints) of water to 68°C (154°F). Stir in the pilsner malt and Carapils. Take the saucepan off the heat, put the lid on and leave to stand for about 15 minutes. Separate out the malt (see page 25).

Add cold water to bring the total volume of liquid in the pan to 4.5 litres (10 pints). Set over the highest heat and add the spraymalt. Stir until all the lumps are gone. Bring to the boil, then carefully add 1 tablespoon Perle. Continue to boil for 15 minutes, then add 1 tablespoon Perle and 1 tablespoon Tettnanger. Leave to boil for a further 15 minutes, then leave to cool in the saucepan (see page 26).

Once the wort has cooled to 20°C (68°F), transfer it to the fermentation vessel using a strainer and funnel. Ensure that all equipment is disinfected. Add the yeast to the fermentation vessel and shake. Attach the fermentation lock to the silicone stopper, fill the airlock and push the stopper into the vessel. The yeast temperature should be maintained at 9–15°C (48–59°F).

Day 14 – Bottling
Prepare a primer and follow the bottling instructions (see page 30). The beer will be ready to drink after another 14 days.

Facts
Style: Pilsner
Bitterness: Low
Goes with: Almost anything if served chilled
Alcohol content: 5%

Ingredients
Malt
200 ml (7 fl oz/scant 1 cup) pilsner malt
200 ml (7 fl oz/scant 1 cup) Carapils
500 g (1 lb 2 oz) spraymalt

Hops
2 tablespoons Perle
1 tablespoon Tettnanger

Yeast
½ packet of Fermentis W-34/70

Primer
100 ml (3½ fl oz/scant ½ cup) water
2 tablespoons caster (superfine) sugar

STEAM BEER

Recipes – Autumn (Fall)

In truly orthodox Swedish sauna society, you aren't allowed to drink beer in the sauna regardless of whether it's in a can or bottle. If you really must drink beer, it should be from wooden drinking vessels or possibly plastic cups if the former aren't available. We're not sauna aficionados, so we advocate the practice of drinking beer from the bottle. A beer that is well suited to the sauna is the steam beer. It is a lager beer made using lager yeast, but in the same way as an ale, namely at a higher temperature. The result is a beer with lots of flavour and plenty of carbonation.

Day 1 – Mash, separate and boil
In the large saucepan, heat 1.7 litres (4 pints) of water to 78°C (172°F). Stir in the crystal malt and Vienna malt. Take the saucepan off the heat, put the lid on and leave to stand for about 15 minutes. Separate out the malt (see page 25).

Add cold water to bring the total volume of liquid in the pan to 5 litres (10½ pints). Set over the highest heat and add the spraymalt. Stir until all the lumps are gone. Bring to the boil, then carefully add 1 tablespoon hops. Boil for 45 minutes and then add 3 tablespoons hops. Boil for a further 12 minutes and then add 1 tablespoon hops. Continue to boil for 3 minutes, then leave to cool in the saucepan (see page 26).

Once the wort has cooled to 20°C (68°F), transfer it to the fermentation vessel using a strainer and funnel. Ensure that all equipment is disinfected. Add the yeast to the fermentation vessel and shake. Attach the fermentation lock to the silicone stopper, fill the airlock and push the stopper into the vessel. The yeast temperature should be maintained at 18–20°C (64–68°F).

Day 14 – Bottling
Prepare a primer and follow the bottling instructions (see page 30). The beer will be ready to drink after another 14 days.

Facts
Style: Steam beer or California common
Bitterness: Just right
Goes with: Simple home cooking or on its own
Alcohol content: 5.5%

Ingredients
Malt
400 ml (13 fl oz/1½ cups) crystal malt
200 ml (7 fl oz/scant 1 cup) Vienna malt
500 g (1 lb 2 oz) spraymalt

Hops
5 tablespoons Northern Brewer

Yeast
½ packet of Mangrove Jack's M54

Primer
100 ml (3½ fl oz/scant ½ cup) water
2 tablespoons caster (superfine) sugar

Winter Brewing
*An IPA for the chalet, a punchy
stout, a biscuit stout, a smoky IPA
and a Christmas beer.*

CHALET IPA

Winter is the time to hit the slopes. Regardless of how much sporting activity takes place, it is the chalet – so often the accommodation of choice for this activity – that we love the best. If you want to add a little something extra to your stay at the chalet, you're best to do so by brewing half a crate of Chalet IPA four weeks in advance. If you've done this, you have one (or two) bottles of beer as an incentive to reach the end of the day's sporting endeavours. This drink is best enjoyed while standing around in your long johns, frying meatballs and boiling up some pasta for your friends and family.

Day 1 – Mash, separate and boil

In a large saucepan, heat 1.7 litres (4 pints) of water to 68°C (154°F). Stir in the CaraRed, pale ale malt and rolled oats. Take the saucepan off the heat, put the lid on and leave to stand for about 15 minutes. Separate out the malt (see page 25).

Add cold water to bring the total volume of liquid in the pan to 5 litres (10½ pints). Set over the highest heat and add the spraymalt. Stir until all the lumps are gone. Bring to the boil, then carefully add 2 tablespoons Fuggle. Boil for 45 minutes and then add 2 tablespoons Nelson Sauvin. Continue to boil for 15 minutes and then add a further 2 tablespoons Nelson Sauvin. Leave to cool in the saucepan (see page 26).

Once the wort has cooled to 20°C (68°F), transfer it to the fermentation vessel using a strainer and funnel. Ensure that all equipment is disinfected. Add the yeast to the fermentation vessel and shake. Attach the fermentation lock to the silicone stopper, fill the airlock and push the stopper into the vessel. The yeast temperature should be maintained at 15–24°C (59–75°F).

Day 14 – Bottling

Prepare a primer and follow the bottling instructions (see page 30). The beer will be ready to drink after another 14 days.

Facts

Style: India Pale Ale

Bitterness: High

Goes with: Simple home cooking

Alcohol content: 6.5%

Ingredients

Malt

400 ml (13 fl oz/1½ cups) CaraRed

300 ml (10½ fl oz/1¼ cups) pale ale malt

200 ml (7 fl oz/scant 1 cup) rolled (old fashioned) oats

500 g (1 lb 2 oz) spraymalt

Hops

2 tablespoons Fuggle

4 tablespoons Nelson Sauvin

Yeast

½ packet of Fermentis S-04

Primer

100 ml (3½ fl oz/scant ½ cup) water

2 tablespoons caster (superfine) sugar

OATMEAL STOUT

Recipes – Winter

An oatmeal stout contains surprising ingredients such as oats, and is characterised by being so silky it is almost creamy. Stout is black because you use black malt. The black malt also gives the beer coffee and roasted tones. A great tip to make your beer even silkier is to be a little mean with the primer as you bottle the beer. This means less carbonation, making the beer seem smoother in your throat.

Day 1 – Mash, separate and boil

In a large saucepan, heat 1.7 litres (4 pints) of water to 67°C (153°F). Stir in the chocolate malt and Carafa III, roasted barley and rolled oats. Take the saucepan off the heat, put the lid on and leave to stand for about 15 minutes. Separate out the malt (see page 25).

Add cold water to bring the total volume of liquid in the pan to 5 litres (10½ pints). Set over the highest heat and add the spraymalt. Stir until all the lumps are gone. Bring to the boil, then carefully add 1 tablespoon hops. Boil for 45 minutes and then add 2 tablespoons hops. Boil for a further 15 minutes, add a further 2 tablespoons hops and leave to cool in the saucepan (see page 26).

Once the wort has cooled to 20°C (68°F), transfer it to the fermentation vessel using a strainer and funnel. Ensure that all equipment is disinfected. Add the yeast to the fermentation vessel and shake. Attach the fermentation lock to the silicone stopper, fill the airlock and push the stopper into the vessel. The yeast temperature should be maintained at 15–24°C (59–75°F).

Day 14 – Bottling

Prepare a primer and follow the bottling instructions (see page 30). The beer will be ready to drink after another 14 days.

Facts

Style: Oatmeal stout

Bitterness: Just right

Goes with: Ideal on its own

Alcohol content: 5.5%

Ingredients

Malt

100 ml (3½ fl oz/scant ½ cup) chocolate malt

100 ml (3½ fl oz/scant ½ cup) Carafa III

50 ml (2 fl oz/¼ cup) roasted barley

100 ml (3½ fl oz/scant ½ cup) rolled (old fashioned) oats

500 g (1 lb 2 oz) spraymalt

Hops

5 tablespoons Cascade

Yeast

½ packet of Fermentis US-05

Primer

100 ml (3½ fl oz/scant ½ cup) water

2 tablespoons caster (superfine) sugar

BISCUIT STOUT

The fun thing about brewing beer is that you can experiment endlessly. You can flavour a beer with more or less anything and make it taste good. We love Christmas ginger biscuits (cookies), so we took our best stout recipe and crumbled them in during the brewing process. The biscuit crumbling helps to add the unmistakable scent of ginger biscuit to the beer's aroma. If you want to enhance that ginger biscuit sensation, you can also flavour with ordinary cinnamon, cloves and ginger.

Day 1 – Mash, separate and boil

In a large saucepan, heat 1.7 litres (4 pints) of water to 70°C (158°F). Stir in the roasted barley. Take the saucepan off the heat, put the lid on and leave to stand for about 15 minutes. Separate out the malt (see page 25).

Add cold water to bring the total volume of liquid in the pan to 4.5 litres (10 pints). Set over the highest heat and add the spraymalt. Stir until all the lumps are gone. Boil for 15 minutes, then carefully add 2 tablespoons hops. Continue to boil for a further 30 minutes and then add a further 2 tablespoons hops. Boil for another 5 minutes and then add the sugar. Boil for another 7 minutes and then add the crumbled ginger biscuits. Boil for a further 3 minutes, then leave to cool in the saucepan (see page 26).

Once the wort has cooled to 20°C (68°F), transfer it to the fermentation vessel using a strainer and funnel. Ensure that all equipment is disinfected. Add the yeast to the fermentation vessel and shake. Attach the fermentation lock to the silicone stopper, fill the airlock and push the stopper into the vessel. The yeast temperature should be maintained at 15–24°C (59–75°F). The sugar means that this beer can easily ferment over the brim of your fermentation vessel. It won't change the flavour, but you may want to put the vessel on a plate.

Day 14 – Bottling

Prepare a primer and follow the bottling instructions (see page 30). The beer will be ready to drink after another 14 days.

Facts

Style: Biscuit stout
Bitterness: Just right
Goes with: The month of advent
Alcohol content: 7%

Ingredients

Malt
200 ml (7 fl oz/scant 1 cup) roasted barley
500 g (1 lb 2 oz) spraymalt

Hops
4 tablespoons East Kent Golding

Flavouring
250 ml (9 fl oz/1 cup) brown sugar
5–10 Christmas ginger biscuits (cookies), crumbled

Yeast
1 packet of Fermentis US-05

Primer
100 ml (3½ fl oz/scant ½ cup) water
2 tablespoons caster (superfine) sugar

SMOKED IPA

Recipes – Winter

We love to eat smoked foods, particulary smoked salmon or white fish. When we do, it's amazing to match smoke with smoke. The drink normally associated with smokiness is whisky, but beer can also generate tar aromas and the flavour of charcuterie. *Touché* whisky. Even if you don't eat much smoked food, you should brew this beer. It's stupendous to discover how much smoke flavour you can achieve, not to mention the experience of opening a bag of crushed smoked malt. The aroma is – for want of a better word – magical. What's more, it can be something of a challenge to find good smoked beer in the shops, so it's well worth brewing your own.

Day 1 – Mash, separate and boil
In a saucepan, heat 1.7 litres (4 pints) of water to 70°C (158°F). Stir in the CaraRed and the smoked malt. Take the saucepan off the heat, put the lid on and leave to stand for about 15 minutes. Separate out the malt (see page 25).

Add cold water to bring the total volume of liquid in the pan to 4.5 litres (10 pints). Set over the highest heat and add the spraymalt. Stir until all the lumps are gone. Bring to the boil, then carefully add 2 tablespoons hops. Boil for 15 minutes and then add a further 2 tablespoons hops. Boil for a further 15 minutes, then leave to cool in the saucepan (see page 26).

Once the wort has cooled to 20°C (68°F), transfer it to the fermentation vessel using a strainer and funnel. Ensure that all equipment is disinfected. Add the yeast to the fermentation vessel and shake. Attach the fermentation lock to the silicone stopper, fill the airlock and push the stopper into the vessel. The yeast temperature should be maintained at 15–24°C (59–75°F).

Day 14 – Bottling
Prepare a primer and follow the bottling instructions (see page 30). The beer will be ready to drink after another 14 days.

Facts
Style: Smoked IPA
Bitterness: Low
Goes with: Smoked fish, cold cuts or on its own
Alcohol content: 5–6%

Ingredients
Malt
300 ml (10½ fl oz/1¼ cups) CaraRed
150 ml (5 fl oz/generous ½ cup) smoked malt
500 g (1 lb 2 oz) spraymalt

Hops
4 tablespoons Cascade

Yeast
½ packet of Fermentis US-05

Primer
100 ml (3½ fl oz/scant ½ cup) water
2 tablespoons caster (superfine) sugar

CHRISTMAS BEER

Recipes – Winter

The most important thing about brewing a Christmas beer isn't which type you choose, but making sure to brew it with plenty of time to spare. It isn't just for the big day itself, but also for the weeks beforehand. This means it's well worth planning your Christmas beer in good time. If you opt for a stout, you may want to start even earlier, as it often needs more time to mature than something like an IPA. This one is especially fun to brew. The base is a brown ale, a style that is well suited to this beer – a little bready and almost a little crunchy in character. We've also chosen to add spices after boiling the hops. The beer will smell 100 per cent Christmassy when you open the bottle.

Day 1 – Mash, separate and boil
In a large saucepan, heat 1.7 litres (4 pints) of water to 67°C (153°F). Stir in the crystal malt, Carafa III and chocolate malt. Take the saucepan off the heat, put the lid on and leave to stand for about 15 minutes. Separate out the malt (see page 25).

Add cold water to bring the total volume of liquid in the pan to 4.5 litres (10 pints). Set over the highest heat and add the spraymalt. Stir until all the lumps are gone. Bring to the boil, then carefully add 1 tablespoon East Kent Golding. Boil for 15 minutes and then add 2 tablespoons Liberty. Boil for a further 13 minutes before adding the teabag filled with Christmas spices. Leave to boil for 2 minutes before removing the bag. Leave to cool in the saucepan (see page 26).

Once the wort has cooled to 20°C (68°F), transfer it to the fermentation vessel using a strainer and funnel. Ensure that all equipment is disinfected. Add the yeast to the fermentation vessel and shake. Attach the fermentation lock to the silicone stopper, fill the airlock and push the stopper into the vessel. The yeast temperature should be maintained at 15–24°C (59–75°F).

Day 14 – Bottling
Prepare a primer and follow the bottling instructions (see page 30). The beer will be ready to drink after another 14 days.

Facts
Style: Brown ale
Bitterness: Just right
Goes with: Christmas
Alcohol content: 5%

Ingredients
Malt
800 ml (1¾ pints/2½ cups) crystal malt
100 ml (3½ fl oz/scant ½ cup) Carafa III
100 ml (3½ fl oz/scant ½ cup) chocolate malt
500 g (1 lb 2 oz) spraymalt

Hops
1 tablespoon East Kent Golding
2 tablespoons Liberty

Flavouring
a selection of whole Christmas spices in an empty teabag (e.g. star anise, Seville orange, cloves and cinnamon)

Yeast
½ packet of Fermentis S-04

Primer
100 ml (3½ fl oz/scant ½ cup) water
2 tablespoons caster (superfine) sugar

YOUR OWN BEER RECIPES

Just like cooking, it's fun to experiment and compose your own recipes for beer you'd like to brew. It's nothing to be afraid of. If you follow just a few simple guidelines, then everything will be fine.

Six steps to your very own beer

1. Choose which beer style you want to brew. Preferably an ale, an overfermented beer. It's easier to ferment the beer at room temperature than to find somewhere that stays between 8–15°C (46–59°F), which is what you need for underfermented beer.

2. Use this formula for the proportions. A kitchen brew (4–5 litres/8½–10½ pints) should contain 500 g (1 lb 2 oz) spraymalt, 400 ml–1 litre (13 fl oz–2 pints/1½–4 cups) special malt (different types of hard roasted malt), 1–5 tablespoons hops (depending on how much flavour and bitterness from hops you want) and ½ packet of dried yeast (if using Fermentis US-05 or S-04, then you're guaranteed a good outcome as they provide very clean flavours).

3. Check the colour of the beer style. The darker the colour, the higher the proportion of roasted malt you need to use. This type of malt is usually referred to as special malt. Try everything from 400–600 ml (13 fl oz–1¼ pints/1½–2½ cups) of special malt in your beer. An example: if you've chosen to make an IPA, start with 400 ml (13 fl oz/1½ cups) caramel malt to 500 g (1 lb 2 oz) spraymalt. This will bring out a beautiful amber colour.

4. Consider whether you want to make a beer that is more inclined towards tropical and citrus fruits, or whether you'd like a beer with grassier, herbier tones. If the former appeals to you, then use American hops such as Citra, Cascade, Mosaic or Amarillo. If you want the earthier alternative, select European hops such as Fuggle, Tettnanger, East Kent Golding or Saaz.

5. Select your yeast. We recommend you keep things simple. Understanding yeast is probably the toughest part of beer brewing. If you stick with dried yeast (such as Fermentis US-05 and S-04) then you have a relatively pure yeast that doesn't flavour the beer to any great extent. This leaves you to work on swapping malts and hops in and out, and starting to learn what combinations do for the flavour and aroma.

6. Here are three tricks you can experiment with to add even more character to your beer. The first is dry hopping. It's not difficult – just carefully remove the silicone stopper after 11 days of fermentation and add some extra hops, berries, herbs or spices. This will add some extra punch to the aroma when you pour the beer.

The second is to flavour the wort itself with berries, herbs or spices. We recommend you add the flavouring 5 minutes before finishing the boil. If you leave it to boil for too long, there is a risk of an odd bitterness to the beer instead of a clear flavour. Your creativity sets the boundaries: try everything from blueberries to juniper twigs, or why not gorgonzola (although maybe not).

The third trick is the easiest (but also the most dangerous) – increasing the alcohol content in the beer by adding sugar. Be careful. It can be tempting to pour lots of sugar into the mix. The risk is you end up with a beer that tastes like a spirit, which is normally not desirable.

Flavouring

You can flavour beer with more or less anything in this wonderful world. Don't forget to disinfect the ingredients through pasteurisation or by pouring boiling water over your flavourings.

YOUR OWN LABEL

Some are happy once they've brewed, fermented, waited, bottled and waited again. They just want to drink and share their home-brewed beer with their friends. But for others, the brewing and fermenting are just excuses for making a fantastic label. It can be as creatively advanced as you like, or purely functional. In any case, we want to offer a few easy tips for how to make your very own beer labels.

Good to have:

printer

thin paper

scissors

milk

brown glass bottles

Collect bottles

While you're waiting for your kitchen-brewed beer to finish fermenting in your carboy (demijohn), you might as well take the opportunity to collect glass bottles. Brown bottles are best as they protect the beer from external factors such as sunlight. Avoid using transparent bottles. We prefer bottling our beer in 330 ml (11 fl oz) bottles, but it's fine to use 500 ml (1 pint) bottles if you prefer.

Remove the labels

The easiest way to remove the labels from store-bought bottles is to fill the sink with warm water and washing up liquid and leave the bottles to soak for half an hour. The labels should then come away easily or with a little help from a washing-up brush.

Brush with milk

Draw or print a motif on your labels on the thinnest paper you can find. After cutting out the labels, attach them by brushing a little milk onto the back of the label before pressing onto the bottle. Using milk means the label sticks, while being easy to remove for your next batch.

Marker pens

It's also nice to draw or write directly onto the bottle. Buy marker pens in fun colours that adhere to glass and decorate your bottle.

Photos

Some may feel a little inhibited when it comes to making their own labels. While the will may be there, they may not have insane design skills. If so, a good idea is to print decent photos on ordinary, thin paper and attach these to the bottles. Simple and very good-looking.

Bottle caps

Minimalistic but effective – put a personal stamp on your beer with a colourful bottle cap. Caps are available in every colour imaginable from the range of home-brewing stores online. You can even have your own caps produced.

Label your beer

A more functional tip is to mark your beer with facts. This is worthwhile if you want to develop as a brewer. Since it's so easy to brew beer (not to mention fun), you may well end up with a whole assortment of beers after a year or so. When your memory fails and you can't remember which beer had the white cap, and which hops went into that stout with the gold cap, it's useful to have labelled your beer. Mark the label with the following: name, brewing date, bottling date, alcohol content, hops, malt and yeast. Pretty soon, you'll have your own beer library in which to browse.

Paus-ölen
Bryggdatum: 4/5 2015
Tappdatum: 18/5 2015
OG: 1.05
FG: 1.01
ABV: 5.2%
Malt: Flaked barley, rostat korn
Humle: EKG
Jäst: Fermentis Safale US-04

Pilsner
Bryggdatum: 4/4 2016
Tappdatum: 28/4 2016
OG: 1.06
FG: 1.018
ABV: 5 %
Malt: Pilsner, Caramat
Humle: Nelson Sauvin
Jäst: Mangrove M-54

Kölsch
Bryggdatum: 12/9 2016
Tappdatum: 26/9 2016
OG: 1.051
FG: 1.008
ABV: 5 %
Malt: Pilsnermalt, Cara
Humle: Hallertauer
Jäst: Fermentis K-97

India Pale Ale
Bryggdatum: 2/5 2017
Tappdatum: 16/5 2017
OG: 1.065
FG: 1.02
ABV: 6.0%
Malt: Carared, Pale ale
Humle: Citra, Cascade
Jäst: Fermentis Safale US-05

TIPS AND TRICKS

Store the beer upright

Never lay down a kitchen-brewed beer in the fridge. It's best if you always store beer upright. If you do, the yeast sediment will fall and form a neat layer at the bottom. If you gently pour the beer into a glass and skip the last centimetre (½ in) in the bottle, you'll be able to drink an almost crystal-clear beer.

Cold crashing

Many complain that homemade beer is often cloudy. This isn't entirely true; if you – as per the above – store the beer upright and pour it carefully, then it will be clear and beautiful. But there is a way (inspired by real breweries) to minimise any cloudiness. It's known as cold crashing. It involves rapidly cooling the beer in the fermentation vessel to around 0°C (32°F). Put your vessel outside if it's wintertime or in a temperate fridge if you have one (in this case a fermentation vessel made from plastic is preferable to glass). Then it should be left until it has finished clearing. This may take a week or so. Subsequently, you oxygenate the beer as usual with primer. If it's still hazy after that, you just have to give up and accept that beer can be cloudy and delicious at the same time.

Dishwasher

Bottling can often be messy. Or at least, it can be if you don't use the dishwasher trick. It's quite simple. If you have a dishwasher. You open the door to the dishwasher when you are bottling the beer from saucepan to bottle, and simply stand the bottles on the inside of the lid. This means that any spills end up in the dishwasher instead of on the floor.

Disinfect the yeast packet

It can't be said enough times that hygiene is incredibly important when brewing beer. Yet there are many who don't disinfect the yeast packet. How are they to know? But if there's one thing that's vital to the beer-brewing process, it's yeast. If the yeast gets infected, then it's all a dead loss. That's why it's well worthwhile pouring a little disinfectant into a glass of water and dipping the packet in it. Also, rinse the scissors you are going to use to open the packet in the disinfectant.

Brew with a friend

One of the most important tips. Kitchen brewing can be seen as a hobby where you learn to make your own beer. But it can also be a social tool. Kitchen brewing is a great way to make friends with your neighbour, or can be something to do one evening after work with a colleague. Even if kitchen brewing works fine on your own, it's more fun when there's two of you.

Oats

Is your beer a bit light on flavour? Try adding oats to your next brew. Add 100–200 ml (3½–7 fl oz/scant ½ cup–scant 1 cup) of oats while mashing. The oats will give the beer a little more body, as well as a wonderful mouth feel.

Thicker foam

Do you want a thicker foam head on your beer? Add 100 ml (3½ fl oz/scant ½ cup) wheat malt to the mash and you'll get foam.

Had enough of kitchen brewing?

If you have a glass fermentation vessel, do the following: add soil. Buy a bag of meadow flower seeds and add to the vessel. Add some more soil. Insert the silicone stopper. Put the vessel in a position out of direct sunlight and wait a few weeks. Beautiful, isn't it?

Troubleshooting

Normally you're very satisfied when you brew your own beer. But should the beer fail, we've gathered together some frequently asked questions and the best responses.

I'm not sure whether my beer is fermenting

The first time you brew beer, it can be tricky to know whether the beer has begun to ferment or not. Most often, the aggressive fermentation occurs some time in the first 36 hours, and only for a few hours at that. After the aggressive phase, the fermentation mostly continues at a calmer tempo, sometimes so calm you barely notice it. The surest way to check whether the beer has finished fermenting is to use a hydrometer. This allows you to check the sugar density prior to fermentation and after. This will also tell you what alcohol content the beer has. The very easiest way to check whether fermentation is still occurring is to see whether the airlock is still bubbling. The bubbles may be separated by intervals of up to a minute, so make sure to watch for a couple of minutes.

The beer tastes good, but it isn't carbonated

This is because the yeast hasn't eaten the sugar added during bottling, and has therefore not produced any carbonic acid. Here are a few tips on how to rectify this unhappy situation:

1) It may be that the primer (the sugar layer) has not mixed properly. The solution in this case is to roll the bottle around so that the sugar fully mixes with the yeast in the beer.

2) Have you had the beer in the fridge or somewhere else too cold prior to bottling? If so, put the bottles somewhere warmer – around 20°C (68°F).

3) If you've tried the two options above without success, then there's only one thing left to – and it's the most awkward. Ensure you fully disinfect your hands. Carefully open the bottle caps. Add 2 tablespoons of caster (superfine) sugar to each (330 ml/11 fl oz) bottle and put on new (disinfected) caps. Hope for the best!

There's a lot of sediment at the bottom of my bottles

The most common reason for this is that you've been careless during bottling. In simple terms, slightly too much of the sediment that has gathered at the bottom of the fermentation vessel during fermentation has made it into the bottles. The solution is to be more careful next time you are bottling, and to ensure that as little sediment as possible makes it into the bottles. Another trick is to buy Protafloc (a clarifying agent) from a home-brewing store and to add it to the brew during the final 5 minutes of boiling the wort. The clarifying agent binds all the debris that gathers in the beer during the brewing process. It's important to note that the sediment isn't hazardous.

The beer tastes watery/wishy-washy

This probably indicates that efficiency during the brewing process has been lower than required, which means that not enough of the sugar from the malt has made it into the wort. When there is insufficient sugar in the wort, the yeast doesn't have enough sugar to eat to produce alcohol in the beer during fermentation. As the alcohol is a platform for flavour, the taste also suffers for this reason. Try using more malt types, as well as more malt, the next time you brew. Alternatively, you can add about 100 ml (3½ fl oz/scant ½ cup) of ordinary caster (superfine) sugar or liquid honey in the final 5 minutes of the wort boil to increase the sugar content in the wort.

The beer tastes of yeast or almost like caramel

This is because the fermentation hasn't worked the way it should. It hasn't successfully removed something known as diacetyl. Response: Leave the beer to stand for a little longer.

Glossary

If you end up in conversation with another brewer, it may be helpful to know what the following words actually mean.

Clone

A clone is a variation on a recipe. You start with a basic recipe that you clone, i.e. you adjust or change it a little to create a completely different variant.

Dry hopping

A way of giving the beer an extra punch of hops and fruit. In practical terms, you pour in lots of hops when the beer has fermented for 1–2 weeks.

Hop cones

The flower on the hop plant. If you decide to grow your own hops, make sure you buy a type suitable for beer brewing and only use the female plants.

Hop pellets

Hop cones that have been ground down and pressed into small pellets. In other words, hop concentrate.

Hop schedule

A table explaining when different hops should be added to the boil.

Hops

A herb used to flavour beer.

Hydrometer

A tool for brewers to measure the alcohol content of beer. You measure the density of sugar prior to and after fermentation.

Malt

In most cases, this refers to the cereal barley, which has often germinated a little before being dried or roasted at various temperatures. The process is called malting and the result is known as malt. The harder you roast, the darker the malt.

Mash

The mixture of crushed malt and warm water. It is in the mash that the starch from the malt is transformed into fermentable sugar, which the yeast then eats to form alcohol.

Secondary fermentation

This is when you leave the wort to ferment for a while longer in a different fermentation vessel. The main reason for doing so is to make the beer clearer and to remove cloudiness. Of course, this is an optional phase in the brewing process.

Whole malt

The name for malt when the grains are whole, unlike crushed malt. If you buy whole malt, you will have to crush the malt yourself.

Wort

The liquid left over once you have separated the crushed malt from the mash. After the yeast has got its teeth into the wort, it turns into beer.

© Jakob Nielsen and Mikael Zetterberg 2017

Original title: Kökosbryggning

First published by Natur & Kultur, Stockholm

The English language edition published in 2018 by Hardie Grant Books, an imprint of Hardie Grant Publishing

Hardie Grant Books (London)
5th & 6th Floors
52–54 Southwark Street
London SE1 1UN

Hardie Grant Books (Melbourne)
Building 1, 658 Church Street
Richmond, Victoria 3121

hardiegrantbooks.com

British Library Cataloguing-in-Publication Data. A catalogue record for this book is available from the British Library.

Kitchen Brewing by Jakob Nielsen and Mikael Zetterberg

ISBN 978-1-78488-183-2

Photography: Fredrik Ottosson
Editor: Henrik Francke
Design: Jakob Nielsen

For the English hardback edition:
Publisher: Kate Pollard
Publishing Assistant: Eila Purvis
Editor: Kay Delves
Proofreader: Emily Preece-Morrison
Translator: Ian Giles
Typesetter: David Meikle
Colour Reproduction by p2d
Printed and bound in China by 1010